# Your Bones

Whiston Worrygoose J & I
Amy Hunter

## Contents

| | |
|---|---|
| All About Bones | 2 |
| Bones in Your Body | 14 |
| Index | 16 |

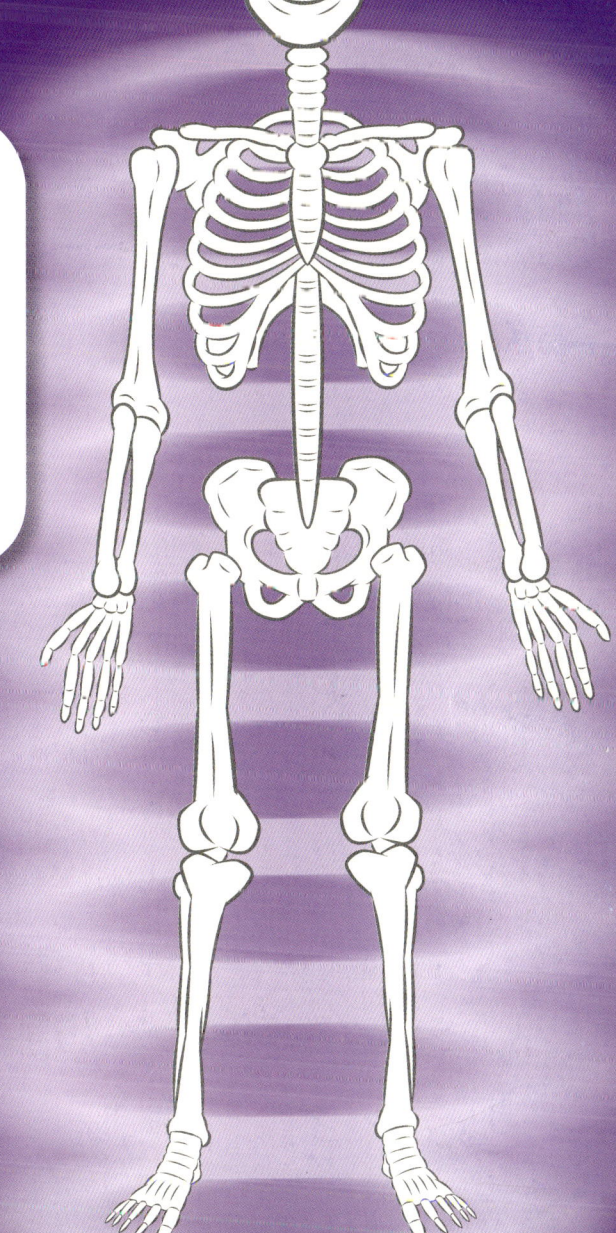

# All About Bones

Hello, I'm Skeleton Sam.
I'm here to tell you all about bones!

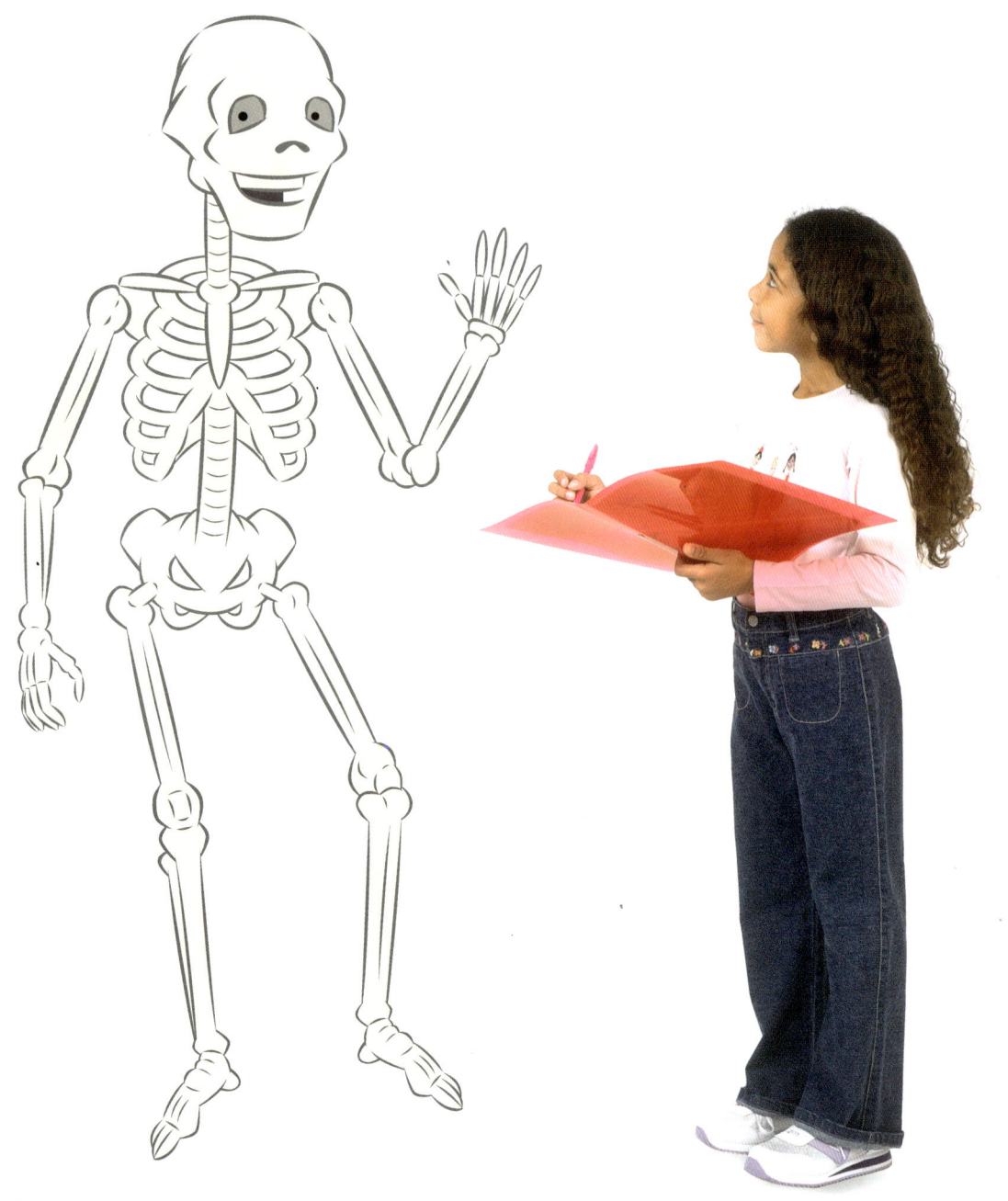

Your bones give your body its shape.
All your bones make up your skeleton.

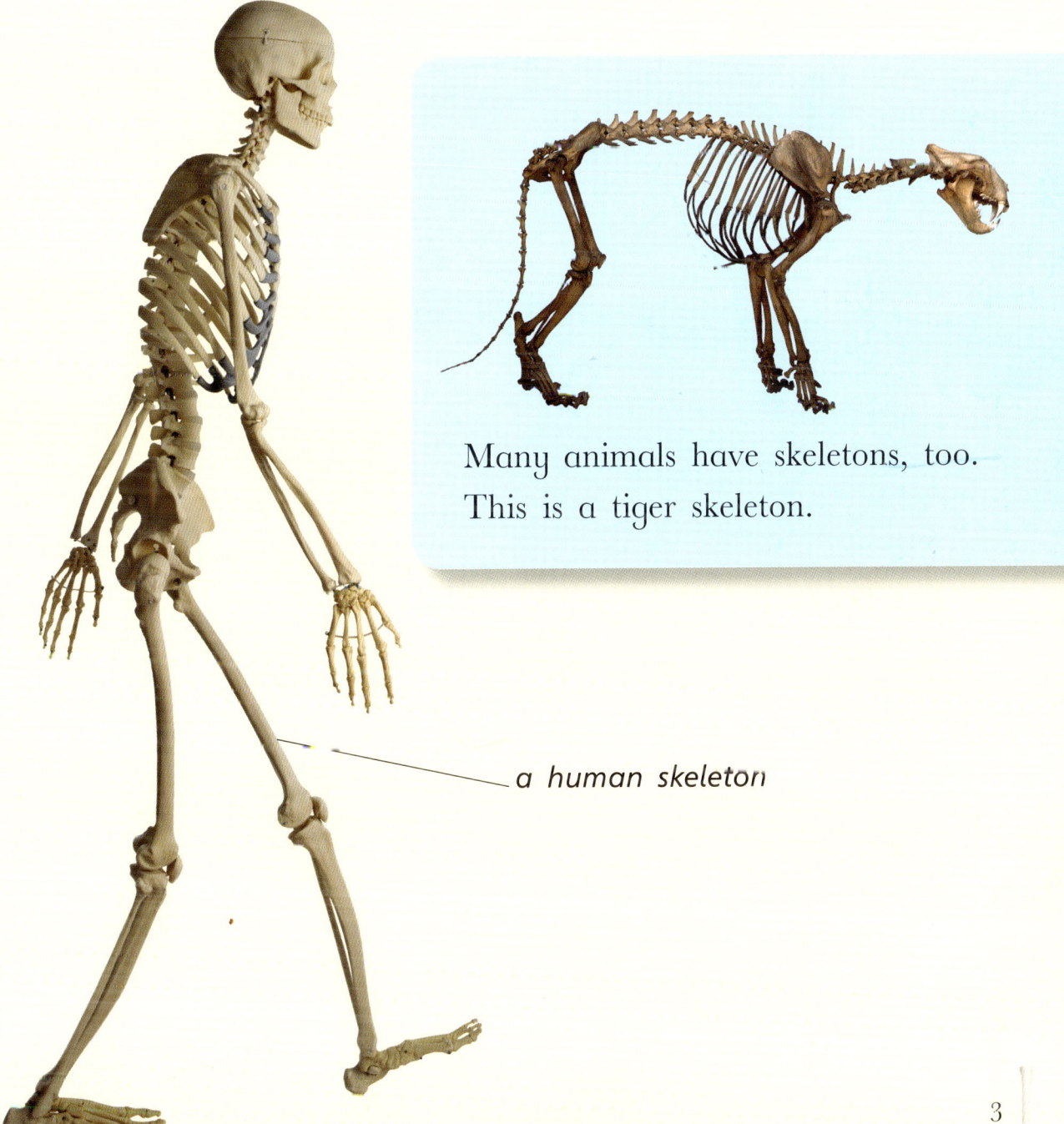

Many animals have skeletons, too.
This is a tiger skeleton.

*a human skeleton*

# How many bones do people have?

An adult has 206 bones.

Oh no, I've lost count!

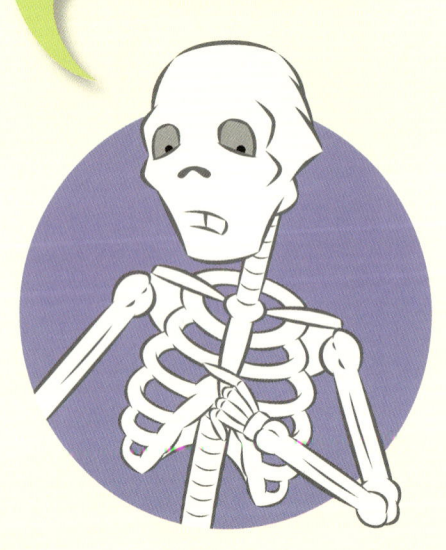

Babies are born with more than 300 bones! When babies grow, some of their bones join together.

## Where is the longest bone in my body?

The longest bone is in your leg. It is called the femur (say fee-muh) or the thigh bone.

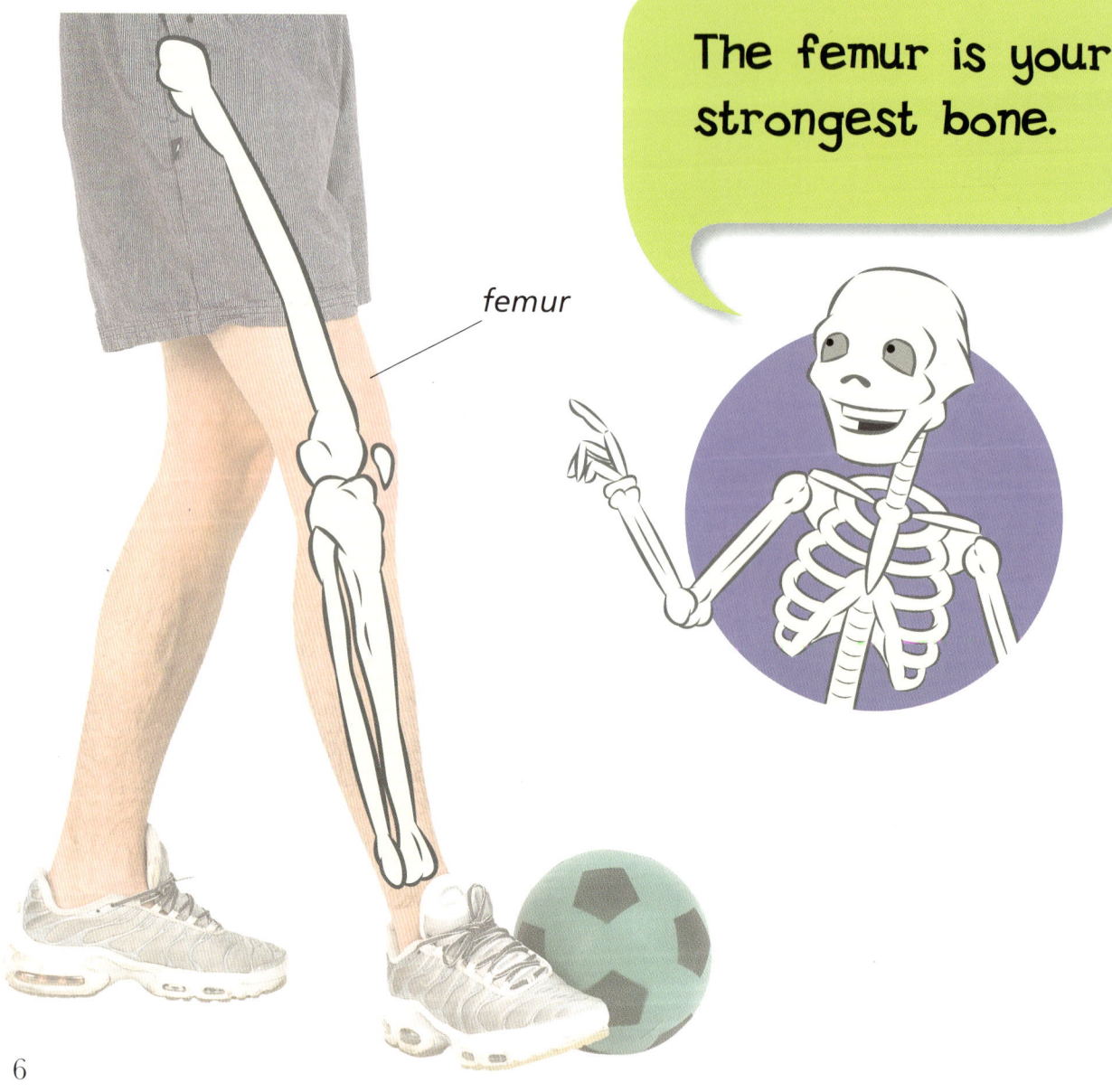

femur

The femur is your strongest bone.

# Where is the shortest bone?

The shortest bone is in your ear.
It is called the stapes (say stay-pes) bone.

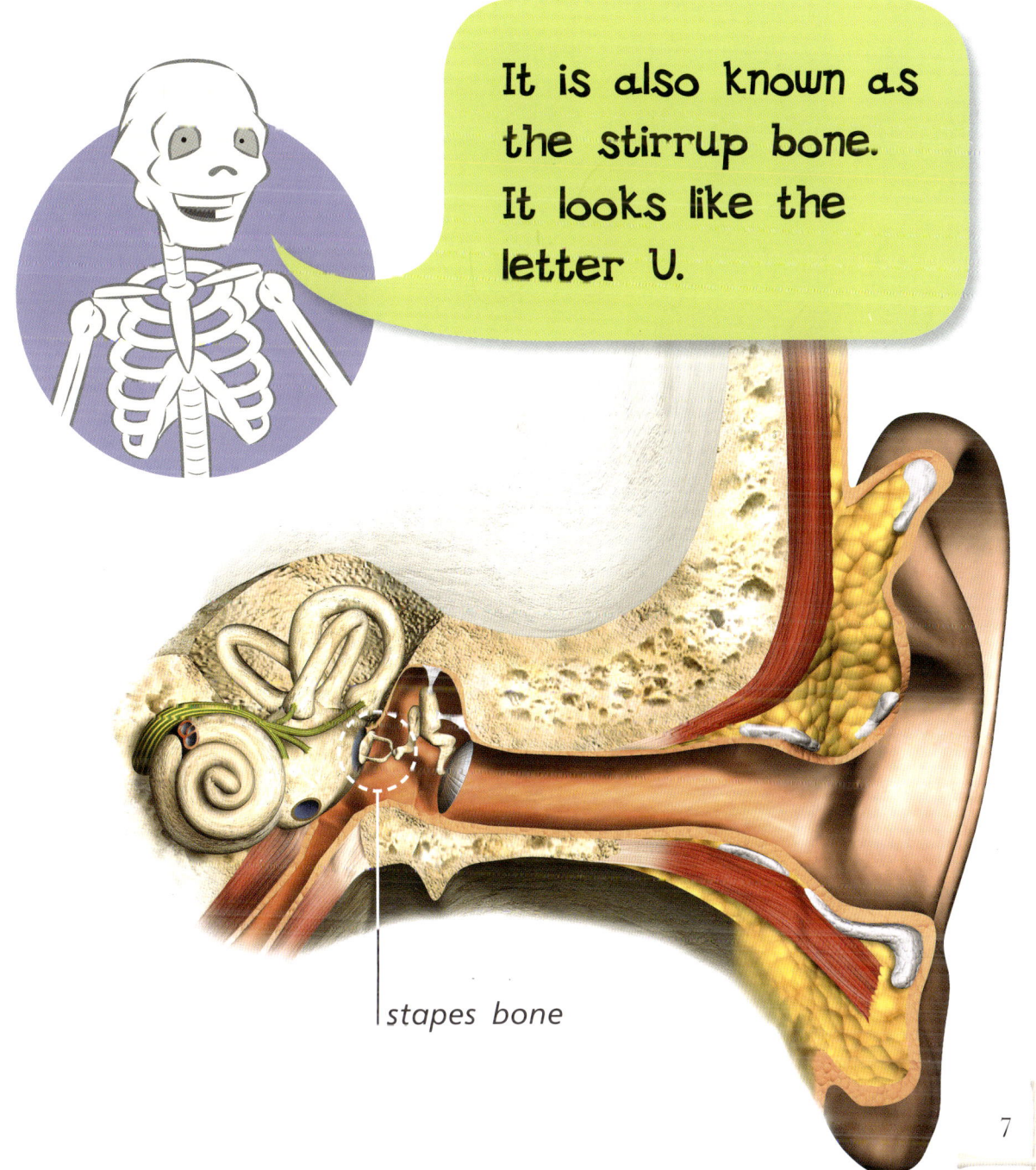

It is also known as the stirrup bone. It looks like the letter U.

*stapes bone*

# Are there more bones in my hand or in my foot?

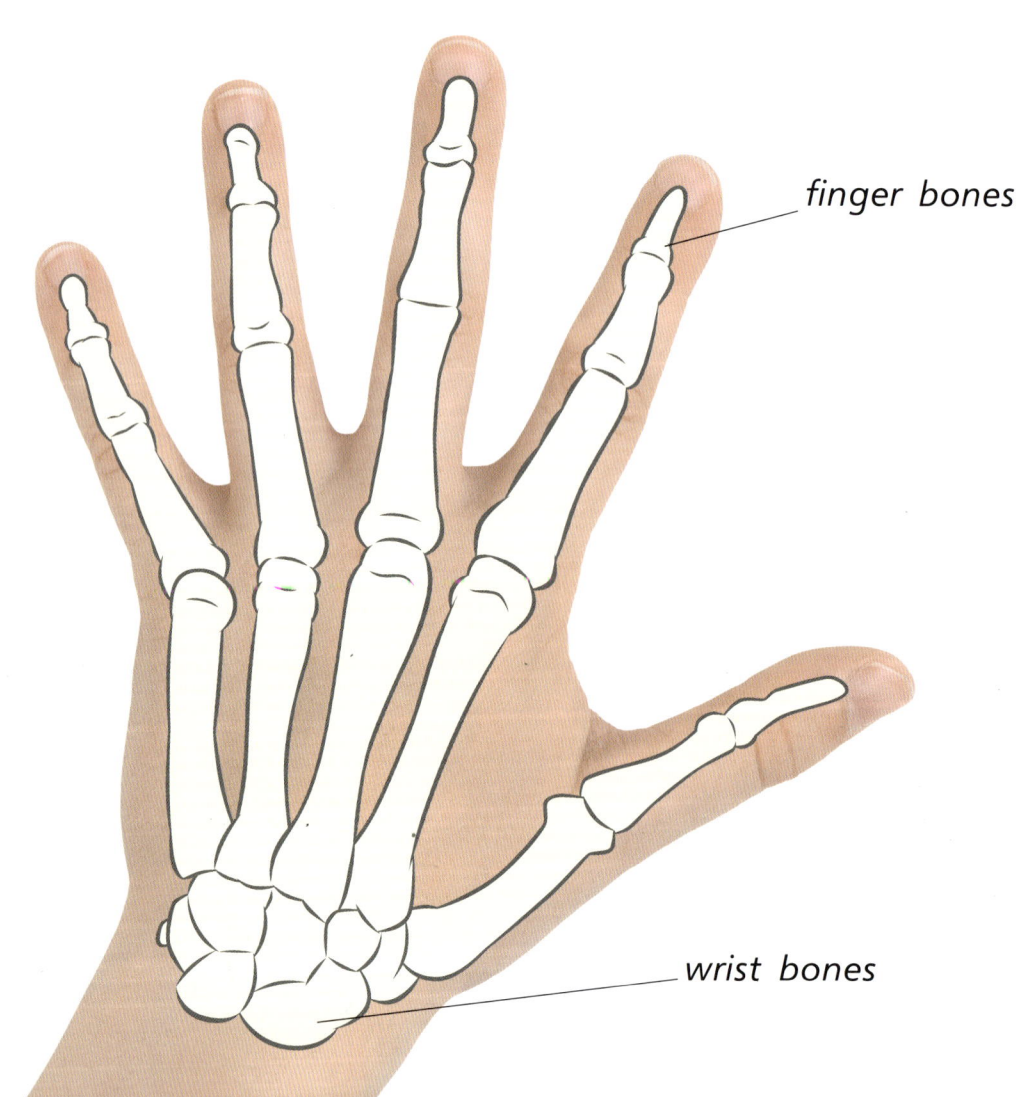

There are more bones in your hand.
Each hand has 27 bones.
Each foot has 26 bones.

*finger bones*

*wrist bones*

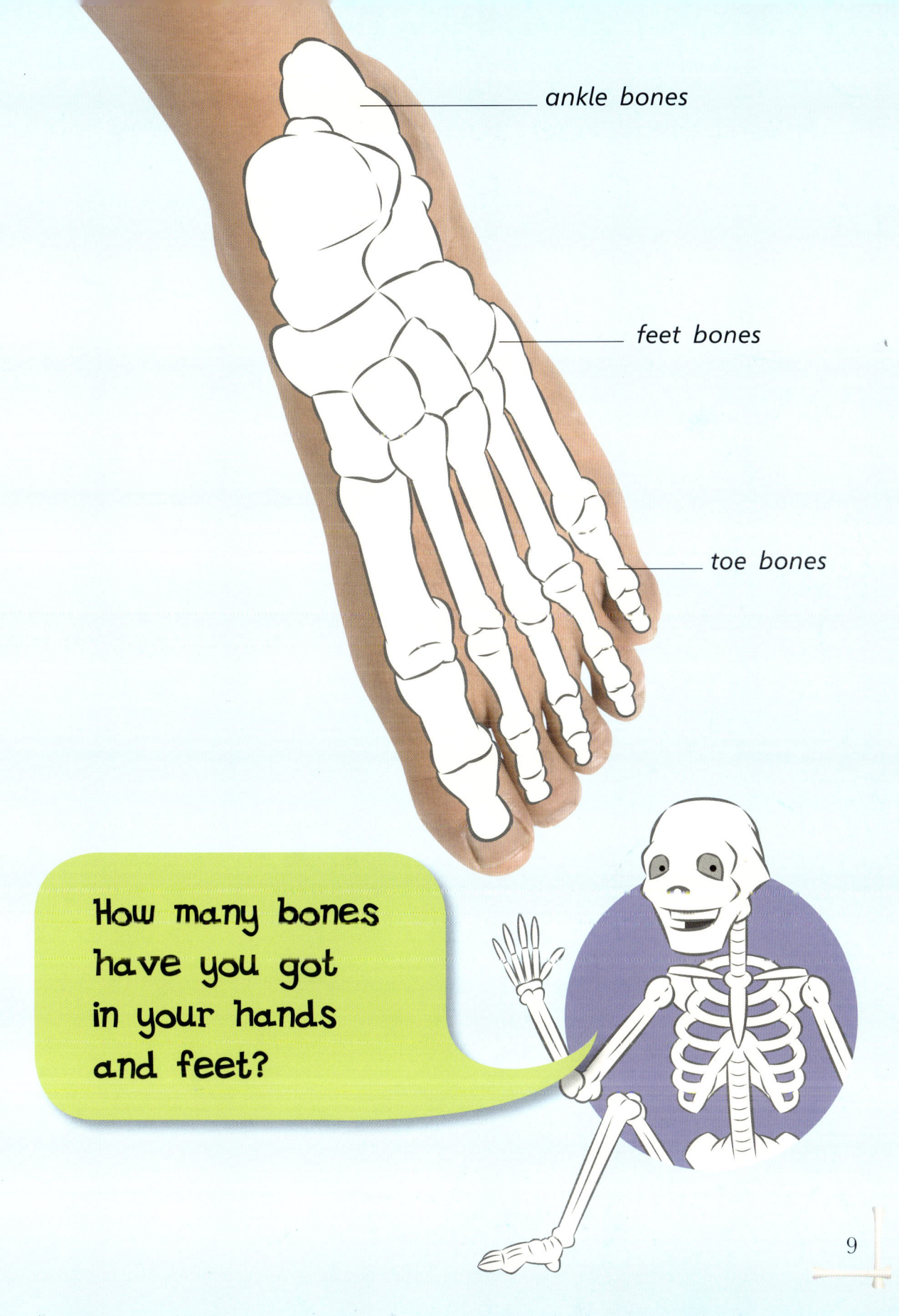

# How can I keep my bones strong?

You can help keep your bones strong by eating good food.

Food that is good for your bones:

milk

yoghurt

spinach

cheese

broccoli

Playing sport also keeps your bones strong.

# What happens when you break a bone?

When you break a bone, you have an x-ray. This helps the doctor to see the break.

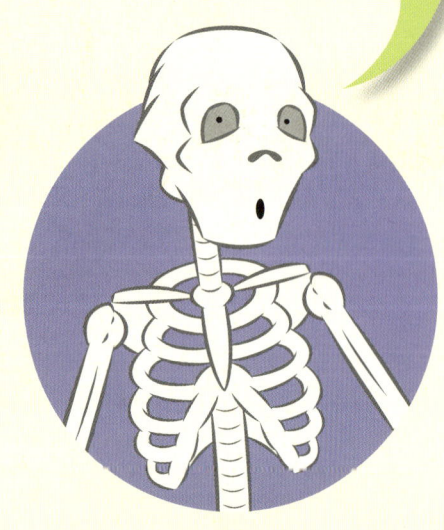

Ouch!

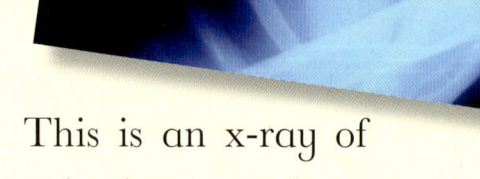

This is an x-ray of a broken arm bone.

Then your broken bone is put into a cast. This keeps your bone very still so it can get better again.

# Bones in Your Body

Wow! We found out a lot about bones!

*skull*

*ribs*

*spine*

*elbow*

Let's look at how your bones fit together.

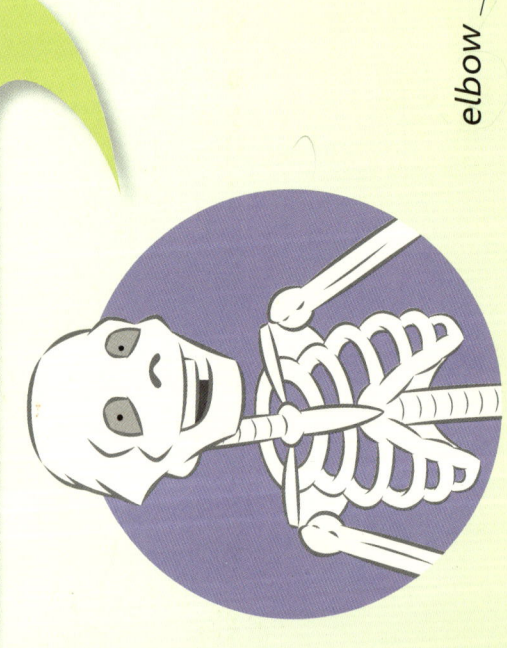

# Index

| | |
|---|---|
| cast | 13 |
| femur | 6 |
| food | 10 |
| skeleton | 3 |
| stapes bone | 7 |
| stirrup bone | 7 |
| thigh bone | 6 |
| x-ray | 12 |

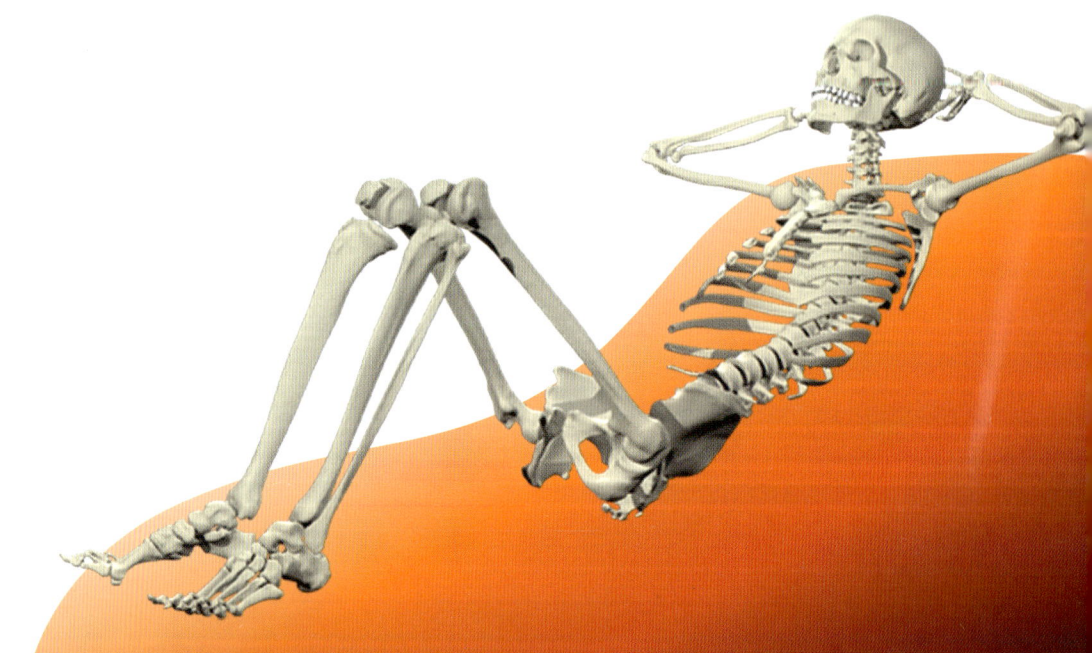